OUR LIVING WORLD

Insects

By **Jenny Tesar**

With Illustrations by Michael Felber

Series Editor: Vincent Marteka

Introduction by John Behler, *New York Zoological Society*

A B L A C K B I R C H   P R E S S   B O O K

WOODBRIDGE, CONNECTICUT

Published by Blackbirch Press, Inc.
One Bradley Road, Suite 205
Woodbridge, CT 06525

©1993 Blackbirch Press, Inc.
First Edition

Printed in Canada

10 9 8 7 6 5 4 3 2 1

Editorial Director: Bruce Glassman
Editor: Geraldine C. Fox
Editorial Assistant: Michelle Spinelli
Design Director: Sonja Kalter
Production: Sandra Burr, Rudy Raccio

Library of Congress Cataloging-in-Publication Data

Tesar, Jenny E.
    Insects / by Jenny Tesar.—1st ed.
        p.   cm. — (Our living world)
    Includes bibliographical references and index.
    Summary: Examines the physical characteristics, senses, metabolism, and life cycle of insects and discusses how they fit into the food chain.
    ISBN 1-56711-037-1   ISBN 1-56711-054-1 (Trade)
    1. Insects—Juvenile literature. [1. Insects.] I. Title. II. Series.
QL467.2.T46   1993
595.7—dc20   92-43714
                                                                          CIP
                                                                          AC

Contents

What Does It Mean to Be "Alive"?

Introduction by John Behler,
New York Zoological Society

One summer morning, as I was walking through a beautiful field, I was inspired to think about what it really means to be "alive." Part of the answer, I came to realize, was right in front of my eyes.

The meadow was ablaze with color, packed with wildflowers at the height of their blooming season. A multitude of insects, warmed by the sun's early-morning rays, began to stir. Painted turtles sunned themselves on an old mossy log in a nearby pond. A pair of wood ducks whistled a call as they flew overhead, resting near a shagbark hickory on the other side of the pond.

As I wandered through this unspoiled habitat, I paused at a patch of milkweed to look for monarch-butterfly caterpillars, which depend on the milkweed's leaves for food. Indeed, the caterpillars were there, munching away. Soon these larvae would spin their cocoons, emerge as beautiful orange-and-black butterflies, and begin a fantastic 1,500-mile (2,400-kilometer) migration to wintering grounds in Mexico. It took biologists nearly one hundred years to unravel the life history of these butterflies. Watching them in the milkweed patch made me wonder how much more there is to know about these insects and all the other living organisms in just that one meadow.

The patterns of the natural world have often been likened to a spider's web, and for good reason. All life on Earth is interconnected in an elegant yet surprisingly simple design, and each living thing is an essential part of that design. To understand biology and the functions of living things, biologists have spent a lot of time looking at the differences among organisms. But in order to understand the very nature of living things, we must first understand what they have in common.

The butterfly larvae and the milkweed—and all animals and plants, for that matter—are made up of the same basic elements. These elements are obtained, used, and eliminated by every living thing in a series of chemical activities called metabolism.

Every molecule of every living tissue must contain carbon. During photosynthesis, green plants take in carbon dioxide from the atmosphere. Within their chlorophyll-filled leaves, in the presence of sunlight, the carbon dioxide is combined with water to form sugar—nature's most basic food. Animals need carbon, too. To grow and function, animals must eat plants or other animals that have fed on plants in order to obtain carbon. When plants and animals die, bacteria and fungi help to break down their tissues. This allows the carbon in plants and animals to be recycled. Indeed, the carbon in your body—and everyone else's body—may once have been inside a dinosaur, a giant redwood, or a monarch butterfly!

All life also needs nitrogen. Nitrogen is an essential component of protoplasm, the complex of chemicals that makes up living cells. Animals acquire nitrogen in the same manner as they acquire carbon dioxide: by eating plants or other animals that have eaten plants. Plants, however, must rely on nitrogen-fixing bacteria in the soil to absorb nitrogen from the atmosphere and convert it into proteins. These proteins are then absorbed from the soil by plant roots.

Living things start life as a single cell. The process by which cells grow and reproduce to become a specific organism—whether the organism is an oak tree or a whale—is controlled by two basic substances called deoxyribonucleic acid (DNA) and ribonucleic acid (RNA). These two chemicals are the building blocks of genes that determine how an organism looks, grows, and functions. Each organism has a unique pattern of DNA and RNA in its genes. This pattern determines all the characteristics of a living thing. Each species passes its unique pattern from generation to generation. Over many billions of years, a process involving genetic mutation and natural selection has allowed species to adapt to a constantly changing environment by evolving—changing genetic patterns. The living creatures we know today are the results of these adaptations.

Reproduction and growth are important to every species, since these are the processes by which new members of a species are created. If a species cannot reproduce and adapt, or if it cannot reproduce fast enough to replace those members that die, it will become extinct (no longer exist).

In recent years, biologists have learned a great deal about how living things function. But there is still much to learn about nature. With high-technology equipment and new information, exciting discoveries are being made every day. New insights and theories quickly make many biology textbooks obsolete. One thing, however, will forever remain certain: As living things, we share an amazing number of characteristics with other forms of life. As animals, our survival depends upon the food and functions provided by other animals and plants. As humans—who can understand the similarities and interdependence among living things—we cannot help but feel connected to the natural world, and we cannot forget our responsibility to protect it. It is only through looking at, and understanding, the rest of the natural world that we can truly appreciate what it means to be "alive."

1

Insects: The Overview

Insects live almost everywhere. Bees fly among flowers in a summer garden. Long columns of army ants advance over the ground in a rain forest. Chinch bugs suck dry young corn plants on a farm. Water bugs hang upside down in a pond. Chewing lice move along the feathers of a bird. Flies crawl over food on a kitchen table.

Insects have inhabited the Earth for more than 350 million years. They were here long before birds, reptiles, mammals, and many other animals. Insects live in more different kinds of places than any other group of animals. Some live deep in caves. Others live on the tops of mountains. Some insects live in hot, dry deserts. Others live in cold, icy Antarctica. Insects live in books and clothes, under tree bark, and even inside other animals.

Insects come in many different sizes, shapes, and colors. All, however, share several common features.

Opposite:
Insects can be found almost everywhere—in books, in clothes, and even inside other animals. Here, an enlarged photo shows a dust mite in a sampling of household dust.

The Body of an Insect

An insect does not have a skeleton of bones inside its body the way humans and other vertebrates do. Its skeleton is on the outside of its body. This exoskeleton ("outside skeleton") is lightweight but strong. It keeps the body from drying out. It also helps to keep out germs, and it provides protection against enemies. An insect's muscles are attached to the inside wall of the exoskeleton.

Every insect body has three parts: the head, the thorax, and the abdomen.

The head is used to find and eat food. Most adult insects have two bulging eyes on the head. These are called compound eyes because they are made up of many tiny lenses. Compound eyes are able to detect movement and color. In addition, most insects have three simple eyes made up of single lenses. These tell the insect if it is day or night.

Insects usually have a pair of antennae on the head, which help them to find food by touch and smell. Antennae come in many sizes and shapes. Some are so short that you can hardly see them. Others are longer than the insect's body. Antennae may look like feathers, threads, strings of beads, or clubs. Mouthparts also come in many different shapes. The mouthparts of a grasshopper are designed for biting off and chewing leaves. Those of a mosquito are designed for piercing the skin and sucking up blood.

The thorax is the insect's locomotion center. That means the thorax is used for moving around. It contains the legs and wings. The thorax consists of three segments. Each segment has a pair of legs, for a total of six legs. Insects are the only animals with six legs. Usually, an insect moves three legs at a time. It moves the front and back legs on one side and the middle leg on the other side. The other three legs rest

The Three Parts of an Insect

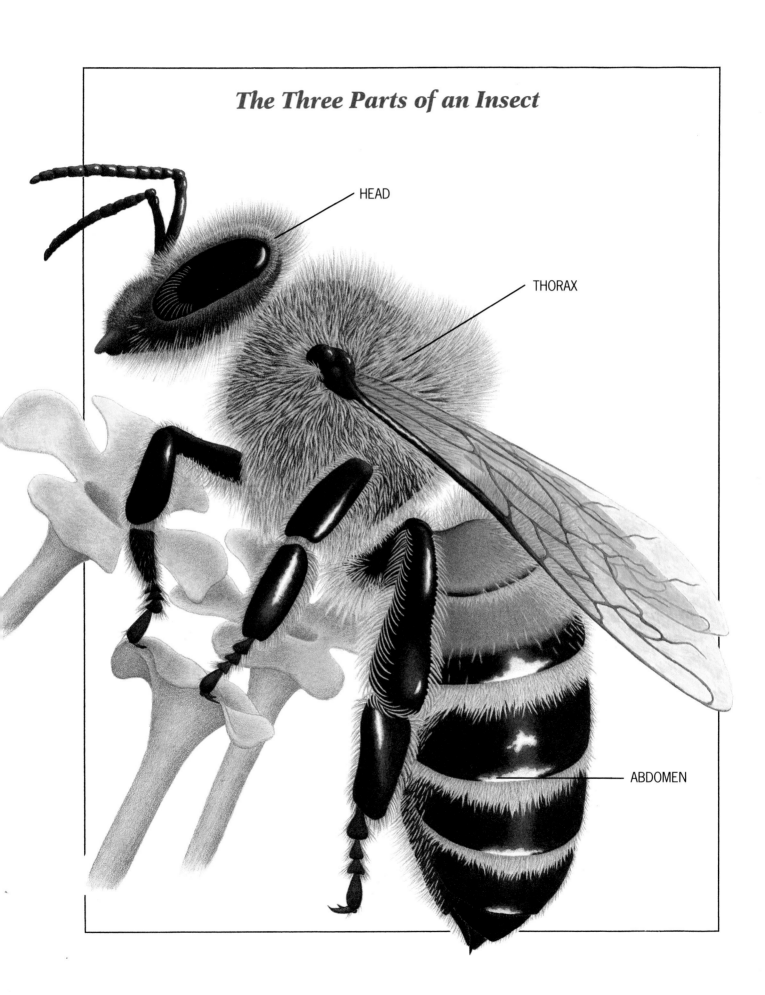

HEAD

THORAX

ABDOMEN

on the ground. They form a triangle that helps the insect keep its balance.

Legs, like antennae and other parts of an insect's body, are designed to help meet an insect's special needs. Insects that dig burrows have front legs that look like shovels. Jumping insects have strong back legs. Swimmers have middle and back legs that look like paddles.

At the end of each leg is a pad surrounded by a pair of claws. The pad is covered with tiny, sticky hairs that make it possible for an insect to walk on walls, windows, and other smooth surfaces. The claws can be used to hook on to rougher surfaces.

Many adult insects also have two pairs of wings on the thorax. Each wing has a network of hollow tubes called veins, which are covered by a thin skin. Mayflies have smooth, transparent wings. The wings of butterflies and moths are covered with many tiny scales. Other insects have wings covered with hairs.

Insects must beat their wings very rapidly when they fly. At top speed, a housefly beats its wings about 180 times a second. That is more than 10,000 times a minute!

A housefly usually flies at a speed of about 5 miles (8 kilometers) an hour. Among the fastest flyers are

What's in a Name?

Earwig

Earwigs are insects with a vicious-looking pair of pincers on the end of their abdomens. An earwig uses its pincers to fight off enemies. No one is certain how earwigs got their name. One theory is that the name comes from an old superstition. Some people believed that the insects liked to crawl into the ears of sleeping people. Another theory suggests the name is a short form of "earwing." When an earwig's wings are spread wide, they have a shape similar to that of a human ear.

There are more than 1,000 kinds of earwigs. Each species has its own scientific name. Earwigs have different common names in English, Greek, Chinese, Swahili, and other languages. But the scientific names are the same all over the world.

hawkmoths and dragonflies, whose speeds have been clocked at more than 30 miles (48 kilometers) an hour!

The abdomen is usually the largest part of an insect. As in humans and many other animals, the abdomen contains the reproductive organs and the organs for digesting food. An insect's abdomen consists of 9 to 11 ring-shaped segments, which make the abdomen flexible.

Many insects have large appendages (body parts attached to other body parts) on the abdomen. These body parts have various uses. A springtail has a tail-like appendage called the furca. When the springtail is resting, special muscles hold the furca in a bent position under the abdomen. When the springtail senses danger, the muscles push the furca against the ground. This helps thrust the insect into the air.

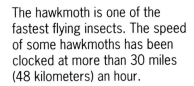

The hawkmoth is one of the fastest flying insects. The speed of some hawkmoths has been clocked at more than 30 miles (48 kilometers) an hour.

The Amazing Variety of Insects

There are more different kinds, or species, of insects than all other animals put together. Scientists have identified more than 750,000 insect species! But the actual number of species is much greater. Up to 10,000 species are discovered each year. Some scientists believe there may be up to 8 million different kinds of insects. Many insects have not yet been identified, because they are tiny and easily overlooked by people. Others live in tropical rain forests and places that have not been well explored by scientists.

Most insects are small. But a few species reach enormous sizes. One of the largest is the atlas moth of Asia. With its wings spread out, it measures 12 inches (30 centimeters) from wingtip to wingtip.

DID YOU KNOW

Old-time Insects

Insects have lived on Earth for more than 350 million years. They were here long before humans and many kinds of other animals. Lots of insects that lived long ago are now extinct—they no longer exist.

What Is It?

Is that creepy, crawly thing you saw on the bedroom floor an insect? There's an easy way to tell: Count the legs. Only insects have six legs.

Many kinds of small animals are mistaken for insects. Some people think that spiders are insects. They aren't. They have eight legs. Centipedes, millipedes, scorpions, and pill bugs are other small animals that aren't insects. They have too many legs.

The giant atlas moth of Asia is one of the largest insects. It has snake-like markings on its wings to scare away predators.

The largest fly is the robber fly of South America. Its body is almost 2 1/2 inches (6 centimeters) long. The largest wasp, a spider-hunting wasp of Brazil, is nearly 3 inches (8 centimeters) long. The longest body of all belongs to certain walkingsticks that live in Asia. They have bodies that are more than 14 inches (36 centimeters) long.

The heaviest insect is the goliath beetle of Africa. It may be 6 inches (15 centimeters) long and weigh more than 3 ounces (85 grams). The heaviest insect that lives in water is the giant water bug of South America. It is 5 inches (13 centimeters) long and weighs nearly 2 ounces (57 grams).

The tiniest insects are very small indeed. The dwarf blue butterfly of South Africa has a wingspan of 1/2 inch (1 centimeter). An ant found in Sri Lanka is 1/30 inch (4/5 centimeter) long. And the fairyfly wasp is even smaller than the period that ends this sentence. Nevertheless, it has three body sections, six legs, and two pairs of wings.

A Collection of Curious Creatures

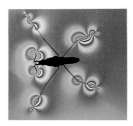

Water strider Look carefully at a quiet pond and you are likely to see water striders skating over the surface. Every so often, one of the striders jumps into the air to catch prey. But neither on takeoff nor on landing does the insect break through the water's surface. A water strider has long middle and back legs. The segments at the ends of these "striding" legs are densely covered with water-resistant hairs. The hairs trap tiny air bubbles that help keep the insect afloat.

Dung beetle Dung beetles often work together to build nests for their offspring. They dig tunnels in the soil. Small dead-end tunnels branch off from the main tunnels. One egg is laid in each of the small tunnels. Then the tunnel is filled with dung, or droppings from other animals. Dung beetles spend much of their lives collecting animal dung. They roll the dung into balls, which they then push into the tunnels. When the eggs hatch, the young beetles, or larvae, feed on the dung.

Monarch butterfly In summer, black-and-orange monarch butterflies are common visitors to gardens in Canada and the northern United States. In fall, as days become cooler, the monarchs leave, flying southward in large groups. Fluttering along at about 10 miles (16 kilometers) an hour, they stop to rest in trees and bushes at night. By the time these frail insects reach their winter homes in California or central Mexico, they have flown 2,000 miles (3,200 kilometers) or more! The monarchs gather in dense, hanging clusters on the branches of certain trees. In spring, they fly north again. During the journey, the females lay their eggs, which develop into the next generation of butterflies. Soon thereafter, the parents die. But here is a mystery: The youngsters fly north, then in fall fly south to the very same trees used by their parents and grandparents. How do they know about those trees?

Orchid mantis The Malaysian orchid mantis is bright pink. Even its eyes and antennae are pink. The mantis spends most of its time in clusters of pink rhododendron flowers, looking exactly like part of the flowers. It sits quietly, not moving for hours on end. It waits until dinner (usually another insect) arrives. Then the mantis shoots out its front legs and quickly grabs its prey. Spines on the legs sink deep into the victim, preventing its escape.

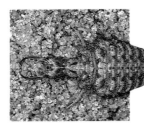

Ant lion Adult ant lions look like dragonflies. Their larvae look like tiny fat worms. These are the "real" ant lions. A larva digs a pit in loose, dry soil. To dig down, it moves backward, going around and around in circles and throwing soil upward, out of the pit. During the digging, the larva constantly tosses its head back and forth to shake off sand that piles up on its head. When the pit is finished, the larva waits at the bottom for an ant to fall in. The larva quickly grabs the ant in its huge jaws. If the ant manages to escape from the jaws, the larva throws grains of soil at it. The unfortunate ant either is buried or falls back into the waiting jaws of the ant lion.

2

The Senses:
How Insects React

 Have you ever tried to catch a housefly with your hands? It's extremely difficult. You have to move very, very fast. A fly constantly pays attention to what is happening in its surroundings. Its big eyes help it sense dangers, such as moving hands and hungry birds. As soon as a fly sees the slightest movement, it reacts. It quickly darts off before it can be caught.

For most animals, eyes and other sense organs provide information about the environment. That is true for insects as well. Any change in the environment that can be detected by an insect's sense organs is called a stimulus. To stay alive, an insect must be able to react to stimuli (more than one stimulus). The insect's reaction to a stimulus is called a response.

In general, a certain stimulus causes a certain response. For example, the fly responds to a swiftly approaching object by flying away from the object.

Opposite:
A dragonfly buzzes through the air. Insects rely on many organs, such as compound eyes, to react to their world.

The Nervous System of a Grasshopper

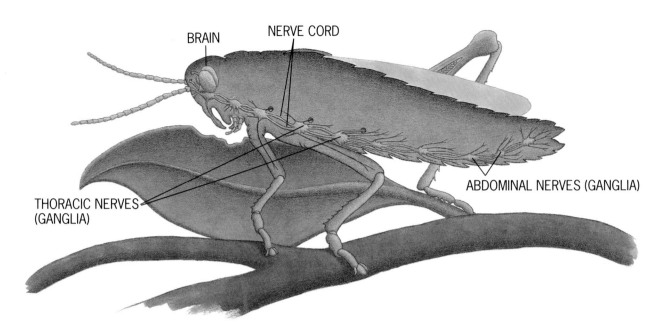

BRAIN

NERVE CORD

ABDOMINAL NERVES (GANGLIA)

THORACIC NERVES (GANGLIA)

An Ancient Dragon

We know about ancient insects from fossils—remains or traces of once-living things. Among these ancient insects was a dragonfly that lived about 300 million years ago. It measured 2 1/2 feet (4/5 meter) from wingtip to wingtip!

This means that the information picked up by a fly's eyes has to be passed to the wings. This job is handled by the fly's nervous system. The nervous system is a system of communication and control. Most animals have a nervous system. This system coordinates the animal's activities, including the way in which the animal reacts to stimuli. Usually, the nervous system is controlled by a brain. The main parts of an insect's nervous system are a tiny brain and a nerve cord that runs from the brain along the length of the insect's body. In humans, the nervous system also includes a brain and a nerve cord (spinal cord). Our cord runs from the brain to the lower back.

Nerve cells in a fly's eyes carry signals to fibers called sensory nerves. The sensory nerves connect to the brain, where the signals are passed down the nerve cord to motor nerves. The motor nerves run out to the muscles that control the wings. They produce a muscular response to the stimulus. The entire process takes only a fraction of a second.

The housefly has other important sense organs that help protect it against a moving threat. Certain

The Senses: How Insects React

hairs on its body are sensitive to changes in air pressure. As your hand moves toward the fly, the hand pushes the air between you and the fly. This movement of air is sensed by hairs on the fly. A message of danger speeds along nerves connecting the hairs to the nerve cord and, from there, to the wing muscles.

Not all nerve fibers in an insect are alike. Those that help an insect to detect danger and escape are much thicker than other nerve fibers. In a fly, the nerve fibers that connect to the wing muscles are very thick. In a grasshopper, the nerve fibers connecting to the back jumping legs are very thick. A grasshopper depends on its back legs to escape enemies.

How Insects See

Flies, grasshoppers, and most other adult insects have a pair of eyes called compound eyes. Compound eyes are made up of tiny light-sensitive parts called ommatidia. Each ommatidium is like a single eye. It has a six-sided lens through which light passes. A nerve runs from each ommatidium to the brain.

Each ommatidium is at a slightly different angle in the compound eye. It picks up light from a slightly different section of the insect's surroundings. The brain combines all the individual images from the

Landing Lights

Insects do not see the same colors that people see. For example, honeybees cannot see red. Red looks like black to honeybees. But honeybees see ultraviolet light, which people cannot see. Honeybees are very sensitive to ultraviolet light. Many flowers that produce nectar have streaks of ultraviolet colors in their petals. These streaks are like the lights along an airport runway. They guide honeybees and other nectar-feeding insects toward the nectar.

The Senses: How Insects React

A great water beetle sits in the water. The larvae of many water beetles have lots of light-sensitive cells on their bodies that help to position them in order to breathe at the surface of the water.

ommatidia to create one complete image, or picture.

The more ommatidia there are in a compound eye, the sharper the complete image. Some ants that live underground have only six ommatidia per eye. A cockroach eye has several hundred ommatidia. The eye of a housefly has about 4,000 ommatidia. Some dragonflies have 28,000 ommatidia in each of their large, bulging eyes. With these eyes, a dragonfly can see almost all around itself. No wonder it is an excellent hunter!

Compound eyes are very useful for detecting small movements. As something moves, its image is picked up by a changing cluster of ommatidia. This immediately alerts the insect that an enemy—or a potential meal—is approaching. However, insects are nearsighted. They see objects clearly only when the objects are nearby. They cannot focus on objects that are more than 2 or 3 feet (about 1 meter) away.

Many adult insects also have small, simple eyes called ocelli. Each ocellus has one lens. Typically, an insect has three ocelli that are arranged in a triangle between the compound eyes. Ocelli probably measure the amount of light in the surroundings. This tells the insect if it is day or night.

Insect larvae have only single-cell eyes. A caterpillar has 12 single-cell eyes grouped in two semicircles on its head.

Some insects have no eyes at all. But they may still have cells that are sensitive to light. For example, the larvae of many water beetles have light-sensitive cells on the tips of their abdomens, near their breathing structures. This helps the larvae position themselves so that the breathing structures are at the surface of

The Senses: How Insects React

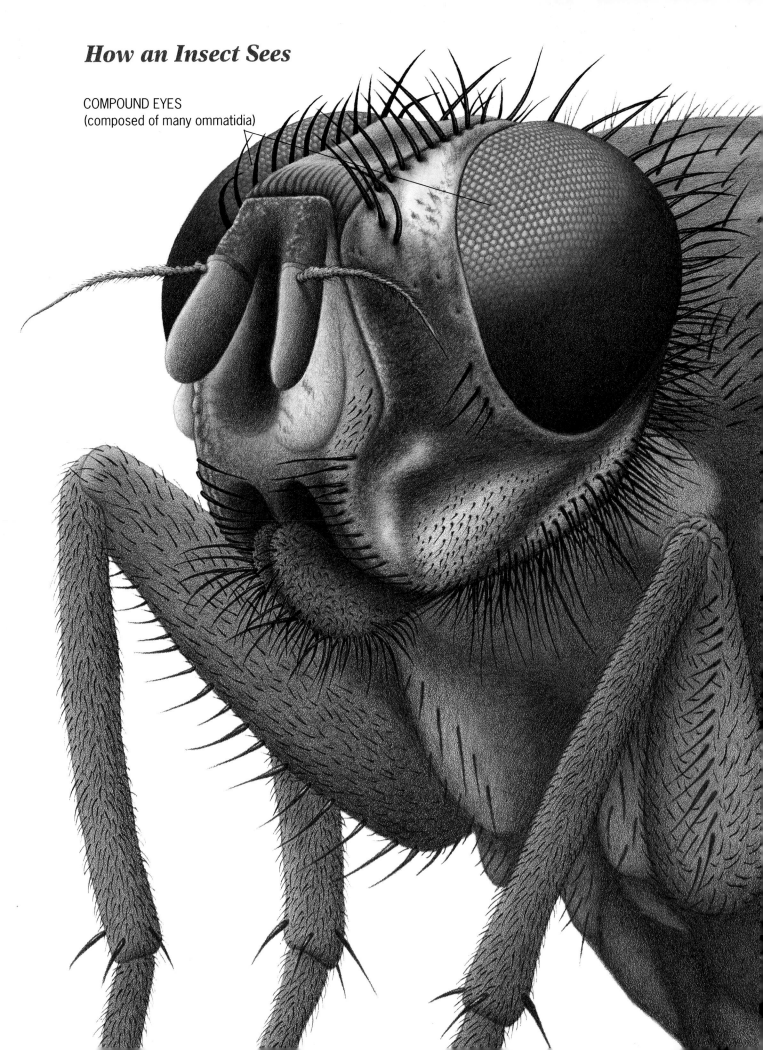

How an Insect Sees

COMPOUND EYES
(composed of many ommatidia)

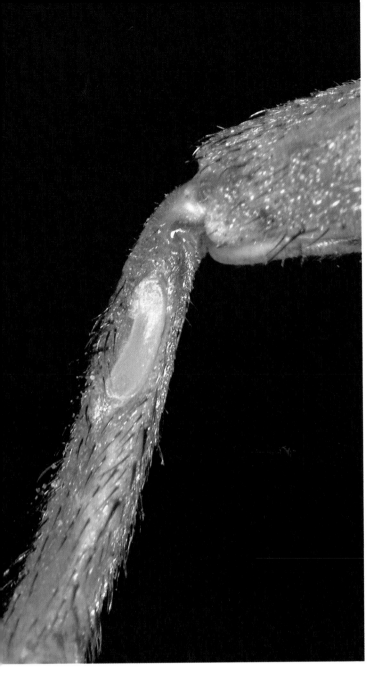

The "ears" of a cricket are located on its front legs. Each ear is an oblong spot that consists of a thin, flat membrane called a tympanum. The tympanum is very similar to the human eardrum.

the water. Although these larvae live in water, they must breathe in air. The light-sensitive cells tell the larvae the direction of sunlight and, therefore, of air.

How Insects Hear

Insects do not have ears on their heads the way humans do. But some insects—including crickets, grasshoppers, and certain kinds of moths—are very sensitive to sound.

Sound is produced by motions called vibrations. An object that vibrates 100 times a second, for example, produces a sound that vibrates at a rate of 100 times a second. We say that sound has a frequency of 100 hertz. Most people can hear sounds between about 16 and 20,000 hertz. Higher sounds are called ultrasonic sounds.

Night-flying owlet moths can detect sounds with frequencies of more than 100,000 hertz. This helps protect the moths against bats. Bats produce ultrasonic sounds in order to locate insects. When owlet moths hear these sounds, they quickly take cover. They dive beneath leaves, where the bats cannot find them.

The two "ears" of owlet moths and short-horned grasshoppers are on each side of the body. The ears of crickets and long-horned grasshoppers are on the front legs. Each ear is an oblong spot that consists of a thin, flat membrane called the tympanum. The tympanum is very similar to the human eardrum. It vibrates when sound waves hit it. The nerve cells that

are connected to the tympanum are stimulated by the vibrations. The nerve cells send messages to the brain, and the insect reacts.

Some insects have antennae or hairs that can sense vibrations. The body of many caterpillars is covered with lots of little hairs. Each hair has a nerve cell attached to its base. Vibrations in the air move the hairs and stimulate the nerves.

Ants seem to be deaf to vibrations in the air, but they are very sensitive to vibrations carried through the soil. Such vibrations are an important means of communication among ants. For example, sometimes the soil caves in and destroys parts of an underground ant nest. Nearby ants make sounds by rubbing together two parts of their bodies. The sound vibrations travel through the ground and are sensed by ants several inches away. These ants hurry to the nest to rescue trapped members of the colony.

The Sense of Smell

Insects do not have noses, but they have an excellent sense of smell. Smell is very important to insects. They use smell to find food, mates, and even places to

Ants use sound as an important means of communication and are very sensitive to vibrations carried through the soil. When an ant is in trouble, it will rub two parts of its body together to send a distress signal to other ants.

21

Male emperor moths have feathery antennae that contain thousands of smell receptors. The antennae are so sensitive that they are able to detect the scent of a female emperor moth from about 2 to 3 miles (3 to 5 kilometers) away.

lay their eggs. Honeybees use smell to identify other members of their colony. All the honeybees that live in one hive have the same scent because they all eat the same food. A honeybee from another hive gives off a slightly different scent. Honeybees that guard the entrance to a hive can smell the difference. They attack strangers that try to enter.

Insects smell with their antennae. Certain cells in the antennae are sensitive to chemicals that make up smells. Generally, the larger or more complex the antennae, the better the sense of smell. Male emperor moths have feathery antennae that contain thousands of smell receptors. These moths can smell the scent given off by a female emperor moth even if she is 2 to 3 miles (3 to 5 kilometers) away!

Some insects have ways to protect their antennae. Certain ants have grooves in the sides of their heads. When their antennae are not in use, they can be folded into the grooves like the antennae of a television.

Other Insect Senses

Taste Like the insect's cells that detect smell, taste organs also detect chemicals. Smell cells detect odor molecules of chemicals; taste organs detect chemicals by actual contact. Some insects have taste organs on their mouthparts or antennae. Others have taste organs on their feet.

Most butterflies taste with their feet. A butterfly depends on its eyes to find nectar-producing flowers. Once it lands on a flower, taste organs in its feet help it find the nectar. The taste organs tell the butterfly when it has stepped into a pool of nectar. Then the butterfly stops and laps up the sweet juice.

Touch All insects have stiff hairs on their bodies that are sensitive to touch. At the base of each hair are one or more nerve cells. When the hair moves, a message is sent along the nerve to alert the insect.

Hairs can sense air currents when an insect is aloft. Hairs tell flying insects which way the wind is blowing.

Antennae also are important organs of touch. Cave crickets have antennae that are much, much longer than their bodies. These antennae probably help crickets find their way in the dark.

Temperature and humidity Sense organs that gather information about the environment's temperature and humidity (amount of moisture) are important organs to many insects. Several kinds of bloodsucking insects have special hairs that sense warmth. These hairs help the insects find birds and mammals, which have blood to feed on. The insects can sense the difference in temperature between their victim's body and the surrounding air.

Most insects have a range of humidities in which they prefer to live. For example, the majority of bloodsucking insects, including body lice, prefer to live on

DID YOU KNOW

Smelly Feet

Did you know that butterflies taste with their feet? They have special taste organs that can taste food and tell the butterfly what to eat!

The Senses: How Insects React

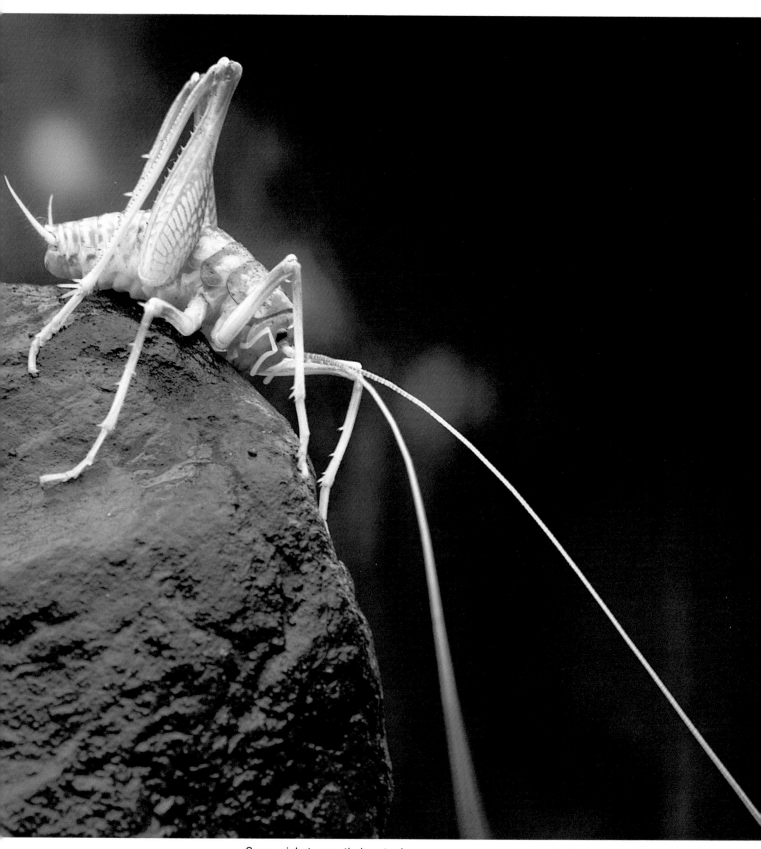

Cave crickets use their extra-long antennae to sense touch. These antennae probably help them find their way in the dark.

The Senses: How Insects React

A flea burrows into the ear of a house cat. Many bloodsucking insects have special hairs that sense warmth. These hairs help the insects locate birds and mammals, which have blood on which they can feed.

moist parts of their host's body. Their sense organs help them find their way from a dry elbow to a damp armpit.

Fancy feelers On the head of an insect is a pair of "feelers," or antennae. Each antenna is made up of segments. Joints between the segments make each antenna flexible. This enables the insect to bend its antennae and wave them around.

Some insects have short antennae with only a few segments. Others have long antennae with more than 100 segments. Antennae come in thousands of different shapes.

Antennae are loaded with various sense organs. For example, each antenna of a male cockchafer beetle contains about 39,000 sense organs!

3

Metabolism: How Insects Function

What's the difference between a stone and a stone fly? Between water and a water beetle? Between silver and a silverfish? Stones, water, and silver are non-living things. Stone flies, beetles, and silverfish are living things. They are insects.

Like all living things, insects perform many chemical activities that are essential to life. Together, these activities are called metabolism. Metabolism involves the storage and use of energy. These functions involve processes such as food getting, digestion, respiration, and excretion. Human metabolism involves these very same functions.

For all living things, the source of energy is food. After an insect eats food, its digestive system breaks down the food into substances that can be used by the body. Its respiratory system (the breathing system) obtains oxygen, which is needed to release energy

Opposite:
Metabolism involves the storage and use of energy, which comes from food. Insects eat a wide variety of foods, including plants and other insects. Here, a praying mantis feeds on a monarch butterfly.

stored in the food substances. Its excretory system removes the wastes produced during metabolism. Does this process sound familiar? These are the same kinds of processes that occur in the human body.

When metabolism functions smoothly, an organism is healthy. It reacts to changes in its surroundings. It grows, it changes from a young animal into an adult, and it reproduces.

When metabolism slows down, the organism does not have enough energy to carry out its normal activities. It lacks the energy needed to fly, chase prey, build nests, and lay eggs.

When metabolism ceases to function, the organism dies. Unlike stones, water, and silver, living things cannot exist without these chemical activities.

What Insects Eat

Insects eat all kinds of things. Many live on liquids, such as blood from animals and nectar from plants. Others catch and kill animals. Still others feed on leaves, roots, and other plant parts. Some insects are scavengers. They eat dead plants and animals. There are also insects that eat substances such as wood, hair, glue, and manure.

It is possible to tell what an insect eats by looking at its mouthparts. There are two main types of mouthparts: chewing and sucking. Chewing mouthparts are designed to hold, bite, and chew food. Sucking mouthparts are designed to suck liquids. There are many variations of these two types of mouthparts.

Grasshoppers, beetles, wasps, and ants have chewing mouthparts that are very similar to those of humans. They grasp food in strong jaws. The jaws move sideways to cut, tear, and chew food and may be extremely powerful. Some beetles can even chew through metals such as lead and zinc!

Butterflies and moths have a long, tube-like tongue that is used to suck nectar from flowers. When the insect is not feeding, the tongue is coiled up on the underside of the head.

Bumblebees have a combination of chewing and sucking mouthparts. They chew into a flower until they reach the nectar. Then they suck or lick the nectar with their short, tube-like tongue.

Cicadas have a grooved beak that contains four needle-like structures. These needles are used to pierce leaves. Then the needles are held together to form two channels. One channel is for ejecting saliva into the leaves to partly digest them. The other channel is used to suck the plant juices.

The tsetse fly feeds on the blood of humans and other large mammals. Tiny teeth on the end of its tongue pierce its victim's skin. Then the tsetse fly sucks up the blood. As the fly feeds, it drips saliva into the blood of its victim. The saliva contains chemicals that prevent the blood from clotting.

Sometimes, the males and females of a species eat different foods. Female mosquitoes feed on blood, but male mosquitoes usually feed on nectar or plant sap.

What an insect eats may change during the insect's life cycle. Young,

Types of Mouthparts

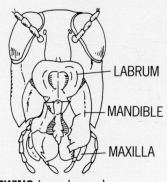

CHEWING (grasshopper)

Insect mouthparts are classified in two broad categories: chewing and sucking. The grasshopper has chewing mouthparts; it bites its food and then chews by moving its mandibles sideways.

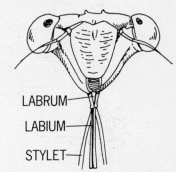

PIERCING-SUCKING (cicada)

In the cicada, the labium, or lower lip, is modified into a grooved beak that encloses four stylets—long, needle-like structures. The cicada uses the stylets to pierce plant tissue and then suck the juice.

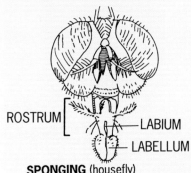

SPONGING (housefly)

The sponging mouthparts of a housefly are suspended from a rostrum, or snout. The mandibles and maxillae are absent; the labium is modified into a tube that ends in two labella—soft, grooved, oval lobes that the fly uses to lap up liquid.

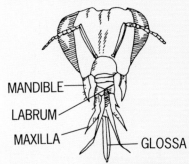

CHEWING-LAPPING (honeybee)

The honeybee has a combination of chewing and sucking mouthparts. The labium is modified into a tongue-like glossa. The bee can bite into a flower and then suck or lap the nectar with its glossa.

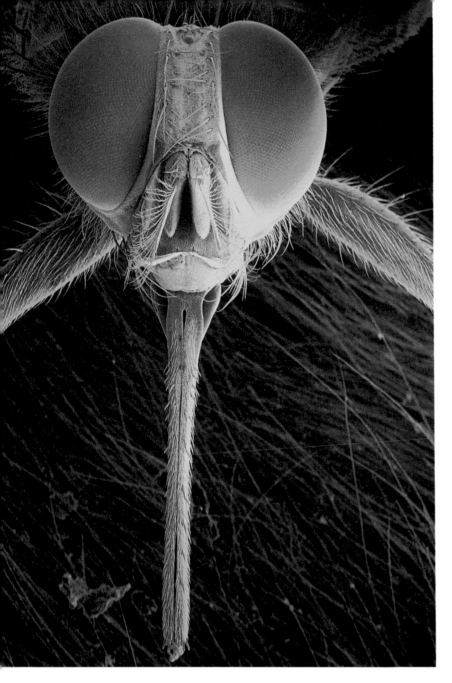

immature insects often eat different foods than adults. Adult butterflies, mosquitoes, and caddis flies suck up liquid foods. But butterfly caterpillars chew leaves. Mosquito larvae have tiny brushes on their heads that sweep bits of dead plants into their mouths. And caddis fly larvae live in the water, where they spin nets to trap small animals.

Some species of midges (a type of fly) and various other insects do not eat as adults. They survive entirely on food reserves that were stored in their bodies when they were young. The sole function of these adults is to reproduce. They live only long enough to mate and lay eggs.

Tsetse flies feed on the blood of humans and other large mammals. They have tiny teeth on the ends of their tongues that pierce skin and enable them to suck up blood through their long mouthparts.

Digesting Food

Before an insect's body can use food, the food has to be broken down. This is done by the digestive system. First, the food is broken down mechanically into tiny pieces by chewing. Then the tiny pieces are broken down chemically.

The digestive system in insects is basically a tube that begins with the mouth. The grasshopper's digestive system is a typical example. After a grasshopper's mouthparts chew leaves, the leaf pieces enter the mouth and travel through the esophagus. The pieces

Metabolism: How Insects Function

The Digestive System of a Grasshopper

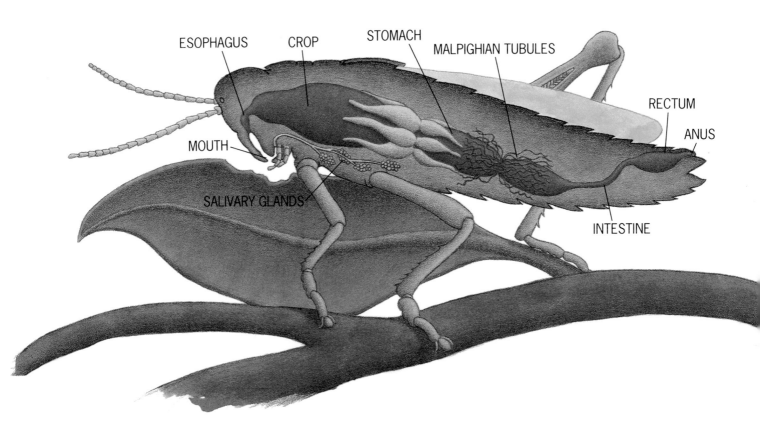

ESOPHAGUS   CROP   STOMACH   MALPIGHIAN TUBULES   RECTUM   ANUS   MOUTH   SALIVARY GLANDS   INTESTINE

enter a large structure called the crop. The crop is a storage chamber. While food is in the crop, it is moistened by secretions from salivary glands. This helps the food pass more easily through the digestive system.

At the end of the crop is the gizzard. The gizzard has tooth-like structures that grind up food into very tiny pieces. The food then moves into the stomach. This is where chemical digestion takes place. Finger-shaped glands pour digestive juices into the stomach. The juices contain strong chemicals called enzymes, which break down the large food molecules into small molecules.

Next, the food moves into the intestine. There, digested food particles plus water pass through the wall of the intestine into the blood. The blood carries

31

them to all the cells of the body. Any undigested materials that remain in the intestine are wastes. They move to the end of the digestive tube and leave the body through the anus.

Getting Oxygen

The exchange of gases between a living thing and its environment is called respiration. An insect takes in oxygen, which is used by every cell in its body to obtain energy from food. During the processes that release energy from food, carbon dioxide is produced. Carbon dioxide is a waste. It must be removed from the cells and from the insect's body.

Most insects breathe through little holes on the sides of their bodies. These holes are called spiracles. The spiracles open into a system of branching tubes

The Respiratory System of a Grasshopper

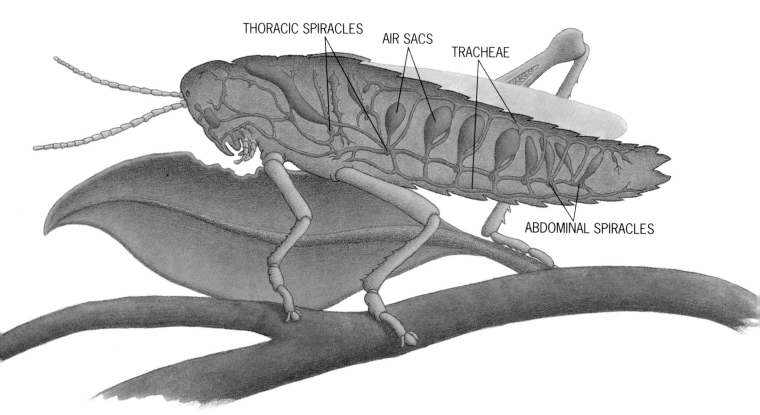

THORACIC SPIRACLES

AIR SACS

TRACHEAE

ABDOMINAL SPIRACLES

called tracheae. Tracheae are found throughout an insect's body—even in its wings. Air enters through the spiracles and moves slowly through the tracheae. In large, fat insects it takes a long time for air to reach all parts of the body. For this reason, large, fat insects cannot move very fast.

Oxygen passes from the tracheae into the cells. Carbon dioxide passes from the cells into the tracheae and then to the spiracles, where it passes to the outside.

Tiny insects and some insect larvae breathe through their skin. Some insects that live in water have gills that absorb oxygen from the water. After oxygen enters through the skin or gills it moves through a system of tracheae.

Removing Wastes

Every living thing produces various wastes during metabolism. The process of removing wastes from the body is called excretion. Carbon dioxide gas is one of the wastes produced during metabolism. It is excreted through the spiracles. Other wastes are excreted through organs called Malpighian tubules.

Malpighian tubules are connected to an insect's digestive tract, where the stomach empties into the intestine. The tubules work like human kidneys. They remove nitrogen wastes from the blood. The wastes are emptied into the intestine. They pass out of the body, together with the undigested wastes, through the anus.

Insect Blood

The circulatory system circulates blood through the body. The main function of blood is to carry nutrients from the intestine to all the cells of the body. It also carries wastes from the cells to the excretory organs.

DID YOU KNOW

I Wood If I Could

Termites eat wood, but they cannot digest wood. The wood is digested by microscopic organisms called protozoa that live inside the termite's intestine. Without the protozoa, the termites would starve to death.

33

Metabolism: How Insects Function

Insects in Disguise

The praying mantis is a master of camouflage.

Many insects often pretend to be something other than what they really are. They use a disguise, or a camouflage, to conceal themselves. This can be extremely useful in getting food.

One master of camouflage is the praying mantis. It is camouflaged by its color, shape, and behavior. The praying mantis is bright green, just like the plants on which it sits. It looks as if it is a part of a plant. It can sit without moving for hours. As it sits, its long front legs are folded in a position similar to that of a human's arms at prayer.

The praying mantis waits...and watches. When another insect comes close, the mantis strikes. Its long, powerful front legs move like lightning to grab the victim. The victim is spiked by sharp spines on the surfaces of the legs. Trapped in a tight grip, the victim is carried by the legs to the mouth. The praying mantis has strong chewing mouthparts. They easily chew through the victim's outer skeleton.

A praying mantis will eat almost anything it can catch, including other praying mantises. Even a baby praying mantis will eat its brothers and sisters. Praying mantises are helpful to humans because they eat beetles, grasshoppers, and many other insects that prey upon crops. The only insects that praying mantises seem to avoid eating are ants.

Metabolism: How Insects Function

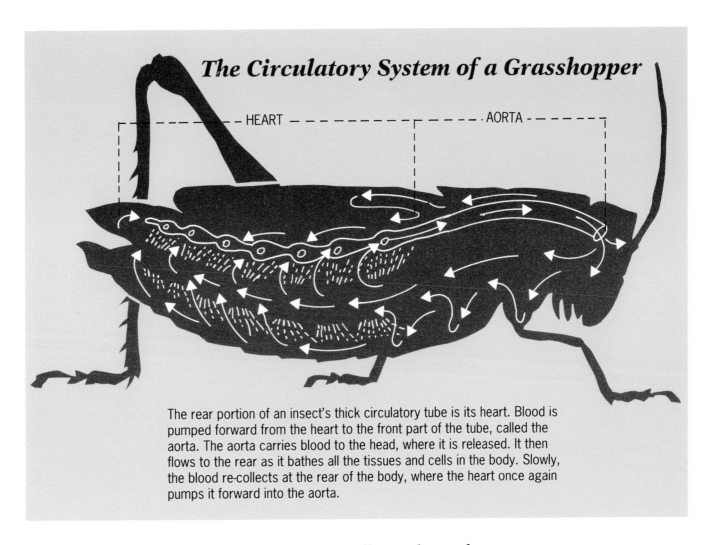

The Circulatory System of a Grasshopper

HEART — — — — — — — — — AORTA — — — — —

The rear portion of an insect's thick circulatory tube is its heart. Blood is pumped forward from the heart to the front part of the tube, called the aorta. The aorta carries blood to the head, where it is released. It then flows to the rear as it bathes all the tissues and cells in the body. Slowly, the blood re-collects at the rear of the body, where the heart once again pumps it forward into the aorta.

In the human body, blood always flows through blood vessels. But in an insect's body, the blood flows out of the blood vessels. An insect's heart is like a thick tube and is located on the rear upper side of the body. It pumps blood forward to the front of the tube, called the aorta, which leads to the head. From the aorta, the blood empties into open spaces in the head. From there it seeps backward to the thorax and abdomen. It bathes all the cells in the body. Then the blood returns to the heart.

Insect blood is usually colorless, but some insects have yellow, green, brown, or red blood. The blood of some insects is poisonous. For example, the blood of blister beetles contains cantharidin. If this poison touches a person's skin, it causes blisters.

Reproduction and Growth

4

It's a warm summer evening. As you walk through a garden, you see tiny flashing lights in the air. The lights are produced by fireflies. There are more than 2,000 species of fireflies, which are actually not flies but beetles. Each species produces its own color of light and rhythm of flashes. The lights are produced in special organs on the lower side of the insect's abdomen.

The purpose of the light display is to attract a member of the opposite sex. When a firefly finds a partner, the two insects mate. Then the female lays her eggs in the soil. About four weeks later, new members of the species hatch from the eggs.

For living things, the process of producing new individuals of the same kind is called reproduction. This is one of life's most important processes. It is necessary for the survival of any species. If members of a species do not reproduce, the species dies out, or becomes extinct.

Opposite:
Reproduction is one of the most important functions for any living thing because it is necessary for the survival of every species. Here, the larger queen honeybee, which lays all the eggs in the hive, is surrounded by a crowd of worker bees.

Fireflies use a flashing-light display to find a mate. Each species produces its own color of light and its own rhythm of flashes.

Meeting a Mate

The first step in reproduction is finding a partner. Fireflies use flashing lights. Other insects use odors or noise to attract mates.

When a female moth is ready to lay eggs, she produces a special perfume. The wind carries the perfume over long distances. You cannot smell this perfume, but a male moth can. He smells the perfume through his feathery antennae, even if he is miles away. He flies through the air, following the trail of scent until he reaches the female.

Male grasshoppers and cicadas that want to find mates make buzzing sounds by rubbing together two parts of their bodies. The sounds are carried through the air to the "ears" of nearby females. Male gnats (small flies) form large groups, or swarms, in the air. As the males "dance," the females hear the whir of their wings and fly to join them. Mosquitoes are also attracted to one another by the hum of their wings.

After insects have found and courted their partners, they are ready to mate. During mating, the male releases sperm. In most species, the male places the sperm directly into the female's body. The sperm fertilize the eggs produced by the ovaries of the female. A fertilized egg contains all the material needed to produce a new member of the species.

On a Chirp Date: Cricket Love Songs

A male cricket doesn't have a voice, but he makes lovely music. When a male cricket wants to attract a female, he "sings" by rubbing his front wings together. The female hears the song through the "ears" on her front legs.

To a human ear, all cricket songs sound alike. But crickets can hear differences. Each species of cricket has its own kind of song. A female field cricket is attracted by the song of a male field cricket. She ignores the song of a male bush cricket or other species that are not her own.

House cricket

A female locust extends her abdomen to twice its normal length in order to lay her eggs in the moist sand. The abdomen of a female insect ends with a structure called an ovipositor, or "egg placer." The female uses her ovipositor to lay eggs deep in the soil or sand.

Laying Eggs

All insects hatch from eggs. Most insect eggs are very small. People usually need a magnifying glass in order to see insect eggs.

Some insects (certain cockroaches and flies, for example) do not lay eggs. Their fertilized eggs stay in the body of the female until they hatch. But most insects lay their eggs. The female's abdomen ends with a structure that is called an ovipositor, or "egg placer." The female uses her ovipositor to lay the eggs.

Different species lay their eggs in different places. Mosquitoes and dragonflies lay their eggs in water. Many butterflies and moths attach their eggs to leaves. Locusts lay their eggs in the soil. The female ichneumon fly uses her sense of smell to locate the larvae of beetles that live in wood. Then she uses her ovipositor to bore through the wood and into the larvae. She lays her eggs inside the larvae. When the ichneumon eggs hatch, the young feed on the beetle larvae.

The Reproductive System of a Female Grasshopper

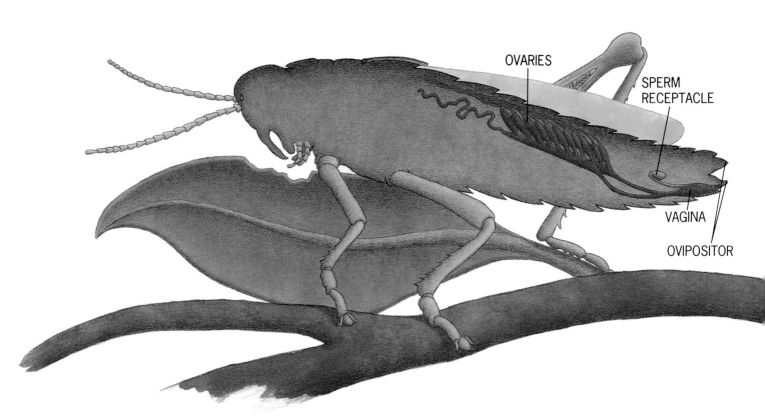

OVARIES

SPERM RECEPTACLE

VAGINA

OVIPOSITOR

Most insects leave their eggs after they are laid. Others take care of the eggs until they hatch. The greatest care is shown by honeybees, termites, and other social insects. Within a colony of social insects the eggs are protected from predators and harmful changes in the environment. The young insects that hatch from the eggs in the colony are also carefully fed and attended.

The number of eggs produced by a female depends on the species. A tsetse fly produces only one egg at a time. Because the fertilized egg remains in the mother fly's body until it is ready to hatch, it has a very good chance of surviving. A female cockroach forms a protective capsule that holds several hundred eggs. She carries the capsule for a while, then puts it in a safe place.

A giant water beetle may lay 1,000 eggs. Most of these eggs do not survive. They are eaten by predators

EGG

NYMPH

NYMPH

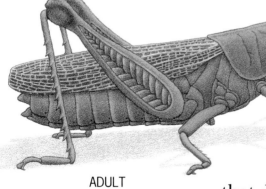

NYMPH

ADULT

Incomplete Metamorphosis

or killed by cold, drying, or other conditions. In a colony of social insects, only one female (the queen) lays eggs. She lays many eggs to maintain the size of the colony. For example, a termite queen may lay up to 3,000 eggs a day—and she may do this for 10 years or more!

Developing in Stages

During their life, most insects go through a series of drastic changes in appearance. Together, these changes are called a metamorphosis. Insects undergo one of two kinds of metamorphosis.

Insects that undergo incomplete metamorphosis, such as dragonflies, grasshoppers, termites, plant bugs, and cockroaches, go through three stages in their life cycle: egg, nymph, and adult. The creature that hatches from the egg is the nymph. It looks somewhat like an adult, but it is smaller, and it lacks wings or some other important feature. As the nymph grows, it gradually develops all of its adult features.

Insects that undergo complete metamorphosis, such as butterflies, moths, ants, bees, and beetles, go through four stages in their life cycle: egg, larva, pupa, and adult.

The egg hatches into a worm-like larva that does not look anything like the adult. This larva has various names, depending on which insect or species it is. The larvae of butterflies and moths are called caterpillars. The larvae of flies are called maggots, and the larvae of some beetles are called grubs.

Complete Metamorphosis

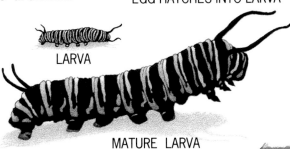

When a larva grows to its full size, it stops eating. It forms a protective case around itself. Within this case, the insect enters the pupal stage. This is sometimes called the resting stage because the insect does not eat or move about. During the pupal stage, both the shape and structure of the insect undergo tremendous changes. The larva slowly turns into an adult. When the adult is fully grown, the pupa case splits open. The insect then pushes its way out of the case and begins to move about in its new form.

EGG HATCHES INTO LARVA

LARVA

MATURE LARVA

Molting

An insect's exoskeleton is made of a hard material called chitin. Unlike human skin, it cannot expand. In order to grow, an insect has to shed its exoskeleton. This process is called molting.

Molting begins when the skin cells secrete a new exoskeleton underneath the old one. The old exoskeleton then splits open and falls off. At first, the new exoskeleton is soft and can stretch. During this time, the insect grows in size, and the new exoskeleton is able to expand with it. Soon, however, the new exoskeleton hardens.

PUPA

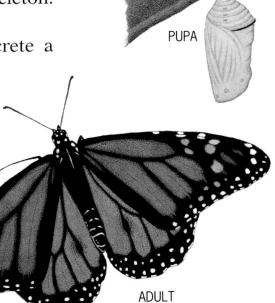

The number of times an insect molts depends on the species. Some insects molt only 3 or 4 times before they are fully grown. Others molt as many as 30 times. Once an insect becomes an adult, it stops molting. Its exoskeleton cannot shed or stretch. It spends the rest of its life in this adult exoskeleton.

ADULT

43

5

Fitting into the Web of Life

Every living thing must be able to survive in its own unique environment. How an organism looks, how its body works, and how it behaves are all connected to the kind of environment in which it must live. An organism's environment is made up of many elements, including the land, food sources, and other living things. In a healthy environment, all these elements create a natural balance for all the things that live together in the same place.

Every insect, like every other living thing, has evolved special characteristics that allow it to survive. A good example is the ladybird beetle, one of the best-loved and best-known insects. Many people call it a ladybug. A ladybird's back looks like a hard shell. It is brightly colored and marked with dots. The "shell" is actually the two front wings. They are very tough.

Opposite:
A ladybird beetle eats an aphid. Many insects are helpful to humans because they are natural predators of insects that destroy valuable plants and crops.

They meet in a straight line down the middle of the beetle's back. They protect the ladybird. When the ladybird flies, it lifts these covers and holds them out of the way of its delicate flying wings.

Ladybird beetles are very helpful to gardeners. They feed on many kinds of aphids and other insects that attack house and garden plants. A ladybug can eat up to 60 aphids a day! Ladybird larvae are also fierce predators. A ladybug larva may eat as many as 25 aphids a day.

A ladybird easily walks up and down stems. It crawls over the tops of leaves and on their undersides. It doesn't fall off, even on windy days. The ladybird has tiny claws near the tips of its legs. These claws help the ladybird cling to stems and leaves. Behind the claws are tiny pads that produce a sticky substance. This helps the ladybird hold on to very smooth surfaces.

With their bright colors, ladybirds are easy to see. That is okay, because they do not have many enemies. Why don't birds and other larger animals eat ladybirds? Ladybirds have a nasty taste. Their bright colors warn enemies to stay away.

In winter, when it is cold, ladybirds hibernate (remain in a resting state). Some ladybirds hibernate alone. But many ladybirds hibernate in large groups. Thousands of ladybirds may cluster together under piles of leaves or in other protected spots.

The ladybird's hard front wings, its dependence on an easy-to-find food supply, the claws and sticky pads on its feet, its nasty taste, and its ability to hibernate during winter are important adaptations that help it survive in its environment.

Neither the ladybird nor any other organism lives in isolation. Every living thing exists within an environment that contains many other living things—and

A Typical Food Chain

A. A butterfly feeds on nectar from a flower.

B. A praying mantis jumps up and eats the butterfly.

C. A snake strikes the praying mantis and eats it.

D. A bird attacks the snake and carries it away to feed its young.

E. When the bird dies, beetles feed on the rotting flesh, helping to decompose the carcass.

Yum-Yum

Insects are an important source of food for other animals. Many fish, such as the mosquito fish, feed on water insects, water larvae, and flying insects that fall into the water. Frogs and toads eat enormous numbers of insects, especially pest insects. One marine toad was seen eating 53 mosquitoes in a minute!

Many reptiles and birds are also big insect-eaters. Agamid lizards easily crush beetles with their strong jaws. Swallows and nighthawks feed only on insects—a nighthawk may eat as many as 1,800 flying ants a day!

The giant anteater uses its strong claws to dig termites and ants out of their nests. Then it uses its long, sticky tongue to pick up the insects. Other mammals that eat insects include bats, armadillos, numbats, and chimpanzees.

Even people eat insects. Cockroaches, locusts, and crickets are an important part of the diets of many Africans. Australian aborigines eat honey ants. People in Thailand eat praying mantises. Like meat from cows and other farm animals, insects contain a lot of protein, which is an essential part of human diets.

many non-living things. All living things depend on their environment for survival.

Eating...and Being Eaten

Every living thing needs energy to survive. In any environment, energy passes from one organism to another as food. This transfer of energy is called a food chain. A food chain describes "who eats what." Insects are an important part of many food chains in the world.

All food chains begin with green plants. Green plants make food. Insects and other animals cannot make food. They must eat something. Some insects feed on green plants. Other insects eat animals that feed on the plants. For example, a butterfly sucks the juices from a nectar-bearing flower. A dragonfly then eats the butterfly. Perhaps a frog eats the dragonfly. Then a snake eats the frog, and a hawk eats the snake. When the hawk dies, beetles eat its flesh. When the beetles die, bacteria break down their bodies. That is one example of a food chain.

Living things in an environment are connected by food chains and food webs. These are descriptions of "who eats what." Here, an anole lizard eats a Jamaican firefly.

Here's another food chain: A cricket eats grass. A chicken eats the cricket. A boy eats the chicken. Bedbugs attack the boy in his bed and feed on his blood. Another bug called the masked hunter eats the bedbugs. A virus disease kills the masked hunter. Then bacteria feed on the dead insect's body.

Most insects eat a variety of foods; they are part of many food chains. For example, the tomato horn-worm, which is the larva of a species of hawkmoth, feeds on tomatoes, potatoes, eggplants, and tobacco. Eating a variety of foods gives the insect a better chance to survive. That way, if one food is missing from the environment, it can eat another.

In every habitat, there are many food chains. These food chains often overlap or connect. Aphids are eaten not only by ladybird beetles but also by lacewing larvae. Crickets are eaten by assassin bugs,

Fitting into the Web of Life

birds, and frogs. A description of how all the different organisms in a habitat feed on each other is called a food web.

Insects Pollinate Plants

One of the most important jobs in the natural world that is performed by insects is pollination. Pollination must take place before a flowering plant can make

Many insects pollinate plants, which is one of the most important roles in the natural world. Various kinds of flowering plants depend on insects for pollination and, therefore, for their reproduction. Here, an elephant hawkmoth hovers in the air as it gathers nectar from a valeriana flower. In the process of feeding, it will pick up pollen on its feet and carry it to the next plant it lands on.

seeds. A flowering plant has two reproductive structures. The male structure produces pollen, which contains sperm. The female structure produces eggs. To form seeds, pollen must be carried from the male structure to the female structure so that the sperm and egg can unite.

Many kinds of flowering plants depend on insects for pollination. These plants often have lots of brightly

Food for Baby

One very important part of a food chain is filled by scavengers. Scavengers feed on dead organisms. Many insects are scavengers. For example, a pair of burying beetles use their sense of smell to locate a dead mouse or bird. Then they roll and push the dead animal to a place where the soil is soft. The beetles bury the body in a shallow hole. Then the female lays her eggs on the body. When the larvae are born, they will feed on the rotting flesh.

colored, sweet-smelling flowers. A bee, butterfly, or other nectar-feeder is attracted by bright colors and strong smells. As an insect crawls over the flower, tiny grains of pollen become trapped on its hairy legs and body. When the insect flies to another flower of the same kind, pollination can take place. The pollen carried on the insect's body from one flower falls onto the sticky female structure of another flower.

By pollinating flowers, insects help themselves as well as the rest of the environment. They ensure that the flowers will make seeds. The seeds will then grow into new plants, which will produce more flowers and more nectar. In many ways, the insects are helping to keep themselves alive while they also help flowers to reproduce.

Insects and Humans: Together in the Natural World

People and insects interact in many different ways. Some insects are called "pests" by people. Insects such as locusts, whiteflies, Colorado potato beetles, and boll weevils destroy large amounts of crops. Gypsy moths kill trees by eating all their leaves. Termites and many beetles feed on wood, including wood used in houses and furniture. The larvae of carpet beetles feed on carpets, sweaters, and fur coats. Although these insects can make life uncomfortable for humans, they are simply doing what they need to do in order to survive. A boll weevil doesn't know it's eating food meant for humans!

Some insects carry microscopic organisms that cause harmful, even fatal, diseases. Yellow fever, malaria, bubonic plague, typhus, and sleeping sickness are among the diseases spread by insects.

People use pesticides to kill "harmful" insects. Unfortunately, these chemicals also kill other

Some insects depend on humans and other large mammals for survival because they feed and reproduce on the bodies of other organisms. Here, an enlarged photo shows a human head that is infested with the eggs of a species of blood-sucking louse.

The Insect Defense: Survival Techniques

Insects defend themselves in many ways. Some insects use camouflage to blend in with their surroundings. Some insects run or fly quickly away. Other insects form protective shells or produce foul-smelling liquids. Still others pretend to be something they're not. Here are several examples:

Fake Bees Bee flies are fat flies that look like bees. They have thick black or gold-brown hair on their bodies. They even buzz like bees. But they do not have stingers. Birds that avoid bees are fooled. They do not attack bee flies.

Ouch! Female bees and wasps have a stinger at the ends of their abdomens. They use the stinger to defend themselves. Many birds that feed on insects avoid bees and wasps. They have learned that these insects can inflict painful stings.

Smoke Screens If a bombardier beetle is attacked, it sets off a bomb! Secretions from several glands in the beetle's body flow into a special sac in the abdomen. When the secretions mix together, they explode. A tiny puff of smoke bursts out of the back end of the abdomen. The smoke blocks the enemy's view while the beetle escapes.

animals. For example, spraying pesticides to kill mosquitoes and gypsy moths has also killed rare butterflies.

Not all insects are pests. Many insects are very helpful to people. Bees make honey and beeswax. Silk is obtained from the cocoons spun by the larvae of the silkworm moth. And many insects provide food for humans around the world.

Protecting Insects

As people have built houses, roads, and various other structures, they have also destroyed important insect habitats. Several species of helpful and beautiful insects have been harmed in the process. Many insect populations are falling. Some of these insects have even become extinct; that is, no more members of the species survive. Among the most endangered insects are many species of butterflies.

Some special groups are working to protect insect habitats. In Pacific Grove, California, a group called Friends of the Monarchs convinced their town to

Clicking Acrobats Click beetles feed on leaves and flowers. If a click beetle is disturbed, it quickly drops to the ground. If it lands on its back, it lies quietly for a few seconds, pretending that it is dead. Then, when it seems safe to move, the beetle presses two parts of its body hard against one another. When it suddenly releases the tension, there is a clicking sound, and the beetle flips high into the air. The beetle repeats this click-and-flip movement until it lands on its feet and can crawl or fly away.

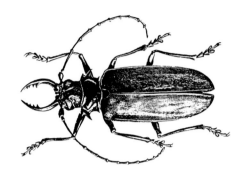

Beyond Be-leaf When a Kallima butterfly flies through the air with its wings open, it is a brightly colored creature—and an attractive sight to a hungry bird. But when this butterfly senses danger, it quickly settles on a branch and claps its wings tightly together. Suddenly, the butterfly looks exactly like a dead leaf. Only the undersides of the wings show. They are pale brown and marked with lines and spots like those seen on a dead leaf. When the butterfly "disappears," the hungry bird, or predator, is confused. What happened to that tasty-looking butterfly? The bird soon gives up the hunt and flies off to find something else to eat.

protect the wintering grounds of the monarch butterfly. Further south, near Los Angeles, another group protects a colony of the rare El Segundo blue butterfly.

Gardeners can attract and help butterflies by growing plants that produce nectar. Butterflies will visit petunias, marigolds, zinnias, and many other easy-to-grow flowers. Instead of using pesticides that harm other life in the environment, gardeners can depend on natural methods of pest control. For example, garden-supply companies sell ladybird beetles and green lacewings. These insects can easily control populations of aphids and other small, soft-bodied plant pests.

Butterflies, bees, and other insects are valuable parts of our natural environment. They also are among the most interesting animals to study. Watch them as they fly through the air, visit flowers, and crawl along leaves and stems. You'll be amazed at how they fit into the fascinating web of life.

Classification Chart of Insects

Kingdom: Animal
Phylum: Arthropoda
Class: Insecta

More than 750,000 species of insects have been identified by scientists. These species are classified in about 30 orders (different scientists use different classification systems). The following are 15 orders for some of the most commonly known insects.

Major Order	Common Members	Distinctive Features
Thysanura "tassel tail"	bristletails, silverfish	wingless; very long antennae; many with three long tails
Ephemeroptera "ephemeral wings"	mayflies	very short life span; excellent flyers; chewing mouthparts
Odonata "toothed"	damselflies, dragonflies	mouth with a beak resembling a tooth; chewing mouthparts; excellent flyers
Isoptera "equal wings"	termites	front and back wings always almost identical in size and shape; social insects; chewing mouthparts
Orthoptera "straight wings"	grasshoppers, crickets, katydids, cockroaches, praying mantises	wings with straight edges; front wings leathery, back wings used for flying; chewing mouthparts
Homoptera "same wings"	aphids, cicadas, tree hoppers, spittlebugs, scale insects, mealy bugs	filmy wings of similar size and thickness; sucking mouthparts
Hemiptera "half wings"	true bugs (stinkbugs, bedbugs, water striders, water boatmen, etc.)	partly leathery, partly clear wings; piercing and sucking mouthparts
Thysanoptera "tassel wings"	thrips	fringed wings; cone-shaped piercing and sucking mouthparts

Major Order	Common Members	Distinctive Features
Neuroptera "nerve wings"	lacewings, ant lions, alderflies, dobsonflies	large transparent or translucent wings patterned with veins ("nerves"); chewing mouthparts
Coleoptera "sheath wings"	beetles, weevils	shield-like front wings; chewing mouthparts
Siphonaptera "siphon wingless"	fleas	wingless; strong legs; piercing and sucking mouthparts
Diptera "two wings"	true flies, gnats, midges, mosquitoes	one pair of wings; piercing and sucking mouthparts
Trichoptera "hair wings"	caddis flies	long, hair-covered wings; sucking mouthparts
Lepidoptera "scale wings"	butterflies, moths, skippers	wings covered with tiny scales; sucking mouthparts
Hymenoptera "membranous wings"	ants, bees, wasps, gallflies, sawflies, ichneumons	membranous wings, sometimes absent; chewing or sucking mouthparts

THE ANIMAL KINGDOM

Porifera SPONGES	Cnidaria COELENTERATES	Platyhelminthes FLATWORMS	Nematoda ROUNDWORMS	Mollusca MOLLUSKS	Annelida TRUE WORMS

Cnidaria:
- Hydrozoa HYDRAS, HYDROIDS
- Scyphozoa JELLYFISH
- Anthozoa SEA ANEMONES, CORALS

Platyhelminthes:
- Turbellaria FREE-LIVING FLATWORMS
- Monogenea PARASITIC FLUKES
- Trematoda PARASITIC FLUKES
- Cestoda TAPEWORMS

Mollusca:
- Polyplacophora CHITONS
- Gastropoda SNAILS, SLUGS
- Bivalvia CLAMS, SCALLOPS MUSSELS
- Cephalopoda OCTOPUSES, SQUID

Annelida:
- Polychaeta MARINE WORMS
- Oligochaeta EARTHWORMS, FRESHWATER WORMS
- Hirudinea LEECHES

Biological Classification

The branch of biology that deals with classification is called taxonomy, or systematics. Biological classification is the arrangement of living organisms into categories. Biologists have created a universal system of classification that they can share with one another, no matter where they study or what language they speak. The categories in a classification chart are based on the natural similarities of the organisms. The similarities considered are the structure of the organism, the development (reproduction and growth), biochemical and physiological functions (metabolism and senses), and evolutionary history. Biologists classify living things to show relationships between different groups of organisms, both ancient and modern. Classification charts are also useful in tracing the evolutionary pathways along which present-day organisms have evolved.

Over the years, the classification process has been altered as new information has become accepted. A long time ago, biologists used a two-kingdom system of classification; every living thing was considered a member of either the plant kingdom or the animal kingdom. Today, many biologists use a five-kingdom system that includes plants, animals, monera (microbes), protista (protozoa and certain molds), and fungi (non-green plants). In every kingdom, however, the hierarchy of classification remains the same. In this chart, groupings go from the most general categories (at the top) down to groups that are more and more specific. The most general grouping is PHYLUM. The most specific is ORDER. To use the chart, you may want to find the familiar name of an organism in a CLASS or ORDER box and then trace its classification upward until you reach its PHYLUM.

Arthropoda / classes:
- Insecta INSECTS
- Chilopoda CENTIPEDES
- Diplopoda MILLIPEDES
- Symphyla, Pauropoda SYMPHYLANS, PAUROPODS

Insecta (orders):

Collembola, SPRINGTAILS	Embioptera, WEBSPINNERS
Thysanura, SILVERFISH, BRISTLETAILS	Thysanoptera, THRIPS
Ephemeroptera, MAYFLIES	Mecoptera, SCORPION FLIES
Odonata, DRAGONFLIES, DAMSELFLIES	Zoraptera, RARE TROPICAL INSECTS
Isoptera, TERMITES	Hemiptera, TRUE BUGS
Orthoptera, LOCUSTS, CRICKETS, GRASSHOPPERS	Anoplura, SUCKING LICE
Dictyptera, COCKROACHES, MANTIDS	Mallophaga, BITING LICE, BIRD LICE
Dermaptera, EARWIGS	Homoptera, WHITE FLIES, APHIDS, SCALE
Phasmida, STICK INSECTS, LEAF INSECTS	INSECTS, CICADAS
Psocoptera, BOOK LICE, BARK LICE	Coleoptera, BEETLES, WEEVILS
Diplura, SIMPLE INSECTS	Neuroptera, ALDERFLIES, LACEWINGS, ANT LIONS,
Protura, TELSONTAILS	SNAKE FLIES, DOBSONFLIES
Plecoptera, STONEFLIES	Hymenoptera, ANTS, BEES, WASPS
Grylloblattodea, TINY MOUNTAIN INSECTS	Siphonaptera, FLEAS
Strepsiptera, TWISTED-WINGED STYLOPIDS	Diptera, TRUE FLIES, MOSQUITOES, GNATS
Trichoptera, CADDIS FLIES	Lepidoptera, BUTTERFLIES, MOTHS

Mammalia (orders):

Insectivora, INSECTIVORES (e.g., shrews, moles, hedgehogs)	Carnivora, CARNIVORES (e.g., cats, dogs, weasels, bears, hyenas)
Chiroptera, BATS	Pinnipedia, SEALS, SEA LIONS, WALRUSES
Dermoptera, FLYING LEMURS	Tubulidentata, AARDVARKS
Edentata, ANTEATERS, SLOTHS, ARMADILLOS	Hyracoidea, HYRAXES
Pholidota, PANGOLINS	Proboscidea, ELEPHANTS
Primates, PROSIMIANS (e.g., lemurs, tarsiers, monkeys, apes, humans)	Sirenia, SEA COWS (e.g., manatees, dugongs)
Rodentia, RODENTS (e.g., squirrels, rats, beavers, mice, porcupines)	Perissodactyla, ODD-TOED HOOFED MAMMALS (e.g., horses, rhinoceroses, tapirs)
Lagomorpha, RABBITS, HARES, PIKAS	Artiodactyla, EVEN-TOED HOOFED MAMMALS (e.g., hogs, cattle,
Cetacea, WHALES, DOLPHINS, PORPOISES	camels, hippopotamuses)

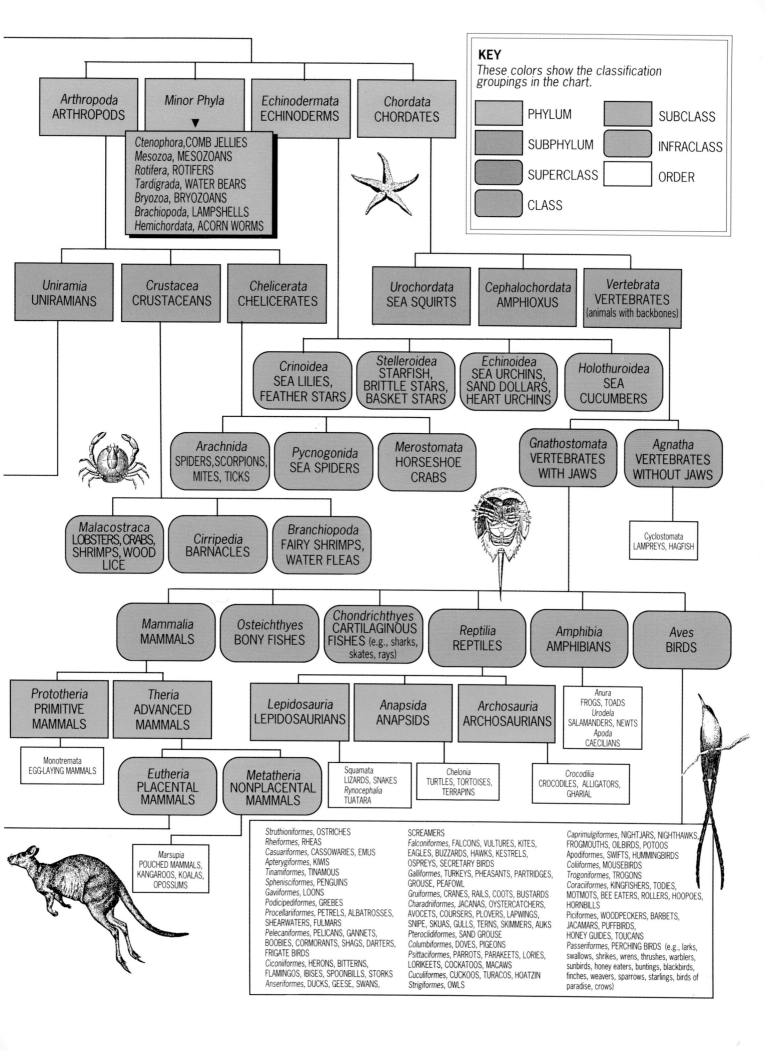

KEY

These colors show the classification groupings in the chart.

PHYLUM   SUBCLASS

SUBPHYLUM   INFRACLASS

SUPERCLASS   ORDER

CLASS

Arthropoda ARTHROPODS

Minor Phyla ▼

Ctenophora, COMB JELLIES
Mesozoa, MESOZOANS
Rotifera, ROTIFERS
Tardigrada, WATER BEARS
Bryozoa, BRYOZOANS
Brachiopoda, LAMPSHELLS
Hemichordata, ACORN WORMS

Echinodermata ECHINODERMS

Chordata CHORDATES

Uniramia UNIRAMIANS

Crustacea CRUSTACEANS

Chelicerata CHELICERATES

Urochordata SEA SQUIRTS

Cephalochordata AMPHIOXUS

Vertebrata VERTEBRATES (animals with backbones)

Crinoidea SEA LILIES, FEATHER STARS

Stelleroidea STARFISH, BRITTLE STARS, BASKET STARS

Echinoidea SEA URCHINS, SAND DOLLARS, HEART URCHINS

Holothuroidea SEA CUCUMBERS

Arachnida SPIDERS, SCORPIONS, MITES, TICKS

Pycnogonida SEA SPIDERS

Merostomata HORSESHOE CRABS

Gnathostomata VERTEBRATES WITH JAWS

Agnatha VERTEBRATES WITHOUT JAWS

Malacostraca LOBSTERS, CRABS, SHRIMPS, WOOD LICE

Cirripedia BARNACLES

Branchiopoda FAIRY SHRIMPS, WATER FLEAS

Cyclostomata LAMPREYS, HAGFISH

Mammalia MAMMALS

Osteichthyes BONY FISHES

Chondrichthyes CARTILAGINOUS FISHES (e.g., sharks, skates, rays)

Reptilia REPTILES

Amphibia AMPHIBIANS

Aves BIRDS

Prototheria PRIMITIVE MAMMALS

Theria ADVANCED MAMMALS

Lepidosauria LEPIDOSAURIANS

Anapsida ANAPSIDS

Archosauria ARCHOSAURIANS

Anura FROGS, TOADS
Urodela SALAMANDERS, NEWTS
Apoda CAECILIANS

Monotremata EGG-LAYING MAMMALS

Eutheria PLACENTAL MAMMALS

Metatheria NONPLACENTAL MAMMALS

Squamata LIZARDS, SNAKES
Rynocephalia TUATARA

Chelonia TURTLES, TORTOISES, TERRAPINS

Crocodilia CROCODILES, ALLIGATORS, GHARIAL

Marsupia POUCHED MAMMALS, KANGAROOS, KOALAS, OPOSSUMS

Struthioniformes, OSTRICHES
Rheiformes, RHEAS
Casuariformes, CASSOWARIES, EMUS
Apterygiformes, KIWIS
Tinamiformes, TINAMOUS
Sphenisciformes, PENGUINS
Gaviiformes, LOONS
Podicipediformes, GREBES
Procellariiformes, PETRELS, ALBATROSSES, SHEARWATERS, FULMARS
Pelecaniformes, PELICANS, GANNETS, BOOBIES, CORMORANTS, SHAGS, DARTERS, FRIGATE BIRDS
Ciconiiformes, HERONS, BITTERNS, FLAMINGOS, IBISES, SPOONBILLS, STORKS
Anseriformes, DUCKS, GEESE, SWANS,

SCREAMERS
Falconiformes, FALCONS, VULTURES, KITES, EAGLES, BUZZARDS, HAWKS, KESTRELS, OSPREYS, SECRETARY BIRDS
Galliformes, TURKEYS, PHEASANTS, PARTRIDGES, GROUSE, PEAFOWL
Gruiformes, CRANES, RAILS, COOTS, BUSTARDS
Charadriiformes, JACANAS, OYSTERCATCHERS, AVOCETS, COURSERS, PLOVERS, LAPWINGS, SNIPE, SKUAS, GULLS, TERNS, SKIMMERS, AUKS
Pteroclidiformes, SAND GROUSE
Columbiformes, DOVES, PIGEONS
Psittaciformes, PARROTS, PARAKEETS, LORIES, LORIKEETS, COCKATOOS, MACAWS
Cuculiformes, CUCKOOS, TURACOS, HOATZIN
Strigiformes, OWLS

Caprimulgiformes, NIGHTJARS, NIGHTHAWKS, FROGMOUTHS, OILBIRDS, POTOOS
Apodiformes, SWIFTS, HUMMINGBIRDS
Coliiformes, MOUSEBIRDS
Trogoniformes, TROGONS
Coraciiformes, KINGFISHERS, TODIES, MOTMOTS, BEE EATERS, ROLLERS, HOOPOES, HORNBILLS
Piciformes, WOODPECKERS, BARBETS, JACAMARS, PUFFBIRDS, HONEY GUIDES, TOUCANS
Passeriformes, PERCHING BIRDS (e.g., larks, swallows, shrikes, wrens, thrushes, warblers, sunbirds, honey eaters, buntings, blackbirds, finches, weavers, sparrows, starlings, birds of paradise, crows)

Glossary

abdomen The section of an insect's body that contains the reproductive and digestive organs.

adaptation The body part or behavior that helps an organism survive in its environment.

aorta A large artery in an insect that carries blood from the heart to the head.

appendage A body part attached to another body part.

camouflage The colors, shapes, or structures that enable an organism to blend with its surroundings.

chitin A hard material found in the exoskeleton of an insect.

compound eyes Two insect eyes made up of many tiny lenses.

crop A storage chamber for partially digested food.

digestion The mechanical and chemical breakdown of food into substances the body can use for growth and energy.

enzyme A substance that breaks down food throughout the digestive system.

esophagus The structure through which food passes from the mouth to the crop.

excretion The removal from the body of wastes that are created during metabolism.

exoskeleton The lightweight but very strong outside skeleton of insects.

extinct No longer in existence.

fertilization The union of sperm and egg, which leads to the development of a new organism.

food chain The order in which a series of organisms feeds on one another in an ecosystem.

food web A system of overlapping and interconnected food chains.

furca A tail-like appendage that is pushed against the ground to spring an insect up into the air.

gizzard The structure at the end of the crop that grinds up partially digested food into very small pieces.

hertz A unit of measurement for sound; the rate of vibration per second of a given object.

hibernate To spend the winter in a resting state.

larva The creature that hatches from the egg of an insect that undergoes complete metamorphosis.

lens A clear structure at the center of the eye through which light passes to the retina.

Malpighian tubules Organs connected to an insect's digestive tract that remove nitrogen wastes from the blood.

metabolism The chemical processes in cells that are essential to life.

metamorphosis The physical development and changes of some insects from egg to adulthood.

molecule The smallest particle of a substance that retains all the properties of the substance.

molting The shedding of an old exoskeleton.

nymph The creature that hatches from the egg of an insect that undergoes incomplete metamorphosis.

ocellus A small, simple eye with one lens.

ommatidia Tiny light-sensitive parts of a compound eye, each with a six-sided lens.

ovipositor A female insect's "egg placer," used to position eggs as they are laid.

pesticides Chemicals used to kill insects that are considered harmful to humans.

pollination The transfer of pollen from the male part of the flower to the female part of the flower; performed by many flying, nectar-feeding insects.

predator An animal that kills other animals for food.

prey Animals that are eaten by other animals.

pupa A casing that protects an insect during metamorphosis from larva to adult.

reproduction The process by which organisms create other members of their species.

respiration The exchange of gases between an organism and its environment; the use of oxygen for the tissues and cells of the body.

scavenger An organism that eats dead plants and animals.

species A group of organisms that share more traits with one another than with other organisms and that can reproduce with one another.

spiracles Holes on the sides of the insect's body through which it breathes.

stimuli Messages received by an animal's senses from its surroundings.

thorax The middle part of an insect's body, which contains the legs and wings.

tracheae Air-conveying tubes found throughout an insect's body.

tympanum A thin, flat membrane that vibrates when sound waves hit it.

ultrasonic sound A high-frequency sound that humans cannot hear.

vertebrate An animal with a backbone.

For Further Reading

Bailey, Jill, and Seddon, Tony. *Animal Movement*. New York: Facts On File, 1988.

Bailey, Jill, and Seddon, Tony. *Animal Parenting*. New York: Facts On File, 1988.

Bailey, Jill, and Seddon, Tony. *Animal Vision*. New York: Facts On File, 1988.

Bender, Lionel. *Poisonous Insects*. New York: Franklin Watts, 1988.

Brooks, Bruce. *Nature by Design*. New York: Farrar, 1991.

Cherfas, Jeremy. *Animal Defenses*. Minneapolis: Lerner Publications, 1991.

Josephson, Judith Pinkerton. *Monarch Butterfly*. New York: Crestwood House, 1988.

Losito, Linda. *Insects and Spiders*. New York: Facts On File, 1989.

Mound, Laurence. *Insect* (Eyewitness Books). New York: Alfred A. Knopf, 1990.

Oram, Liz, and Baker, Robin. *Insect Migration*. Milwaukee: Raintree Steck-Vaughn, 1992.

O'Toole, Christopher. *Discovering Bees and Wasps*. New York: Franklin Watts, 1990.

O'Toole, Christopher. *The Dragonfly over the Water*. Milwaukee: Gareth Stevens Publishing, 1988.

O'Toole, Christopher. *The Honeybee in the Meadow*. Milwaukee: Gareth Stevens Publishing, 1989.

Peissel, Michel, and Allen, Missy. *Dangerous Insects*. New York: Chelsea House, 1992.

Stidworthy, John. *Insects*. New York: Franklin Watts, 1989.

Index

Abdomen, 8, 9 (artwork), 11, 35
Anatomy of an insect
    external, 8–11, 9 (artwork)
    internal, 16 (artwork), 30–35, 31, 32, 35,
        & 41 (artwork)
Ant
    anatomy, 28, 42
    communication, 21 (photo)
Antennae, 8, 21, 22, 23–24 (photo), 38
Ant lion, 13 (photo)
Atlas moth, 11, 12 (photo)

Bat, 20
Bee, 9 (artwork), 17, 22, 36 (photo), 42, 52,
    54, 55
    anatomy, 29 (diagram), 42
Bee fly, 54
Beetle
    anatomy, 28, 42
    diet, 52
    See also Bombardier beetle, Click beetle,
        Cockchafer beetle, Colorado potato
        beetle, Dung beetle, Giant water
        beetle, Goliath beetle, Great water
        beetle, Ladybird beetle.
Blood, 33, 35
Bombardier beetle, 54
Butterfly, 23, 52, 55
    anatomy, 29, 42
    See also Dwarf blue butterfly, El
        Segundo blue butterfly, Kallima
        butterfly, Monarch butterfly.

Caddis fly, 30
Camouflage, 34, 55
Carbon dioxide, 4–5, 32, 33

Caterpillar, 18
Cave cricket, 23, 24 (photo)
Cicada
    anatomy, 29 (diagram)
    mating behavior, 38
Circulation, 33, 35
Click beetle, 55
Cockchafer beetle, 25
Cockroach, 18, 42
    egg laying, 40, 41
Colorado potato beetle, 52
Compound eyes, 8, 15, 17–18, 19 (artwork)
Cricket
    "ear" of, 20 (photo)
    mating behavior, 39 (photo)
    See also Cave cricket.

Deoxyribonucleic acid (DNA), 5
Diet (insect), 28–30
Digestion, 11, 27–32
Dragonfly, 11, 15 (photo)
    anatomy, 18, 42
Dung beetle, 13
Dust mite, 6 (photo)
Dwarf blue butterfly, 12

Earwig, 10 (photo)
Egg laying, 37, 40 (photo)
Elephant hawkmoth, 50–51 (photo)
El Segundo blue butterfly, 55
Emperor moth, 22 (photo)
Excretion, 28, 33
Exoskeleton, 8, 43

Fairyfly wasp, 12
Firefly, 37, 38 (photo)